William T Sleeper

The Rejected King and Hymns of Jesus

A Book for Devotion

William T Sleeper

The Rejected King and Hymns of Jesus
A Book for Devotion

ISBN/EAN: 9783744774659

Printed in Europe, USA, Canada, Australia, Japan

Cover: Foto ©Lupo / pixelio.de

More available books at **www.hansebooks.com**

The Rejected King

—— AND ——

HYMNS OF JESUS

A BOOK FOR DEVOTION.

By Rev. William T. Sleeper.

BOSTON:
LEE AND SHEPARD, PUBLISHERS.
1883.

QUOTATIONS FROM THE NEW TESTAMENT ARE FROM
THE *Revised Version.*

ILLUSTRATIONS FROM BIDA.

Printed by LUCIUS P. GODDARD, *Worcester.*

CONTENTS.

ILLUSTRATIONS.

Jesus by the Sea		*Frontispiece.*
The Return from Egypt	opposite page	18
Jesus in the midst of the Doctors	" "	20
Behold the Lamb of God	" "	26
Healing of the Impotent Man at the Pool	" "	40
Jesus leads the Blind	" "	50
Jesus washes the feet of His Disciples	" "	62
Joseph of Arimathea prepares Christ for Burial	" "	74
Jesus appears to His Disciples	" "	78

THE REJECTED KING.

		PAGE
1.	The Vision	9
2.	The Advent	11
3.	The Guiding Star	14
4.	The Flight	16
5.	The Nazarene	19
6.	The Preparation	22
7.	The Baptism	24
8.	The Ministry	28
9.	The Night Long Prayer	32
10.	In Simon's House	35
11.	Accused of Blasphemy	38
12.	At Bethesda	40
13.	Blasphemed	43
14.	Escaped from the Stoning	46
15.	Besought to Depart	51
16.	At Bethany	55
17.	Weeping over Jerusalem	59
18.	The Last Supper	62
19.	Gethsemane	66
20.	Betrayal and Trial	70
21.	The Crucifixion	74
22.	The Resurrection	78
23.	Room for Jesus	82

HYMNS OF JESUS.

		PAGE
1.	For Me	10
2.	Jesus is Born	13
3.	Beautiful Star	15
4.	Be Not Afraid	17
5.	My Father's Business	21
6.	The Heralding	23
7.	Jesus Comes to Save	26
8.	Where is Jesus?	30
9.	Words of Jesus	34
10.	All from Jesus	36
11.	The Touch of Jesus	39
12.	Come to the Saviour	42
13.	The Love of Jesus	45
14.	The Mind of Jesus	49
15.	At the Feet of Jesus	54
16.	Jesus Whispers	58
17.	Jesus, Advocate	61
18.	Remember Me	64
19.	Jesus Alone	69
20.	Jesus in the Midst	81
21.	Soul, Arise	85
22.	The Believer's Response	86

PREFACE.

I have written this book because it was in my heart, and, like David, I wanted to say: "I have not hid thy righteousness within my heart; I have declared thy faithfulness and thy salvation; I have not concealed thy loving kindness and thy truth from the great congregation."

A little poem out of which the book has grown was published in the *Congregationalist* several years ago, entitled, I believe, "Room for Jesus." A hymn taken from that poem was set to music, and published in "Spiritual Songs for the Sunday-School" by "The Century Co."

I offer this book to the public hoping it may do good.

Rev. G. H. GOULD, D. D., of Worcester, who has read the manuscript, says of it, "I have read 'The Rejected King' with sincere pleasure. It puts the pith of the gospel into a series of rapidly passing *word-pictures*. Their brevity and quick movement kindle a glow of devout feeling which increases to the end."

Rev. A. P. MARVIN, of Lancaster, says: "The poem, as you read it to me, immediately arrested my attention, and held it to the last line. As I am impatient of dull, or diffuse, or tedious poetry, however beautiful the words or the measure,

I concluded the poem had real merit. When I read it over by myself, line by line, and even word by word, spending a day or more over it, my interest was increased, rather than satiated. This is another proof to me of its real merit, and that not as an expression of divine truth, but as poetry."

Rev. D. O. MEARS, D. D., of Worcester, writes me: "I have this morning read with great interest and profit your poems on 'Jesus Rejected.' I do not profess to be a poet, but I do know that there are 'thoughts that burn' scattered over these pages. If you shall cast the work into book form I shall expect that many others will be blessed in the perusal as I have been. I congratulate you on what you have done. The spirit of tenderness breathes in every line."

Mr. HARRY W. FRENCH, the popular writer and lecturer, says: "I have enjoyed *very much* reading and re-reading your poem. I think very highly of it as a production, and hope, for the good of the world, as well as for myself, to see it in print."

With such words as these I am encouraged to send it forth, praying that the blessing of God may rest upon it.

THE AUTHOR.

The Rejected King.

THE VISION.

"He is despised and rejected of men." — Isa. 53:3.

RAPT in what exalted theme
Did the ancient Prophet dream —
Heavenly, or of earth below —
That his soul was set aglow
With a flame of holy fire?
What could wondering seer admire?
'Twas the Mighty One revealed,
But from worldly souls concealed:
Name transcending every name,
Though in lowliness He came;

Beautiful beyond compare,
Yet none saw His beauty rare;
Spurned by those He came to bless,
Hated for His righteousness,
Wounded for our trespasses,
Bruised for our iniquities,
On His head our sins were laid,
By His stripes our peace was made,
Like a lamb to slaughter brought,
Though oppressed He murmured not:
For the world self-sacrificed,
Yet rejected and despised.

FOR ME.

Man of sorrows! can it be
That His sorrow was for me,
 And His agony?

Yes, for me in love He came,
Took upon Himself my blame,
 And endured the shame.

For my fault He insult bore,
Scoffing rude and scourging sore,
 And a thorn-crown wore:

Gave His feet and hands and side,
Gave Himself — my guilt to hide —
 To be crucified.

THE ADVENT.

"There was no room for them in the inn." — Luke 2:7.

In the inn no room for them,
Thy chief guests, O Bethlehem!
Ruth thou gavest room to glean,
David's flocks to crop the green;

But for Mary — blesséd one —
And for David's Royal Son,
Welcome thou dost not provide;
Every room is occupied.

Nobles lounge 'neath lordly domes,
Peasants plod to humble homes,
Foxes in their burrows rest,
Sparrows gather to their nest;
But they give the Heavenly Stranger
For His bed a rugged manger;
Home and grateful cheer for all,
For the Son of God a stall.

O let Bethlehem's children blush!
Let her winds their voices hush!
O'er the silent, star-lit plain
Angels sing a joyful strain —
"Peace on earth, to men good will,
Glory all the world shall fill "—
But it ne'er can be forgot,
Bethlehem's children hear it not.

JESUS IS BORN.

Behold the Lord's salvation
    By poets sung of old,
The hope of tribe and nation,
    By prophets long foretold.
Hosanna, loud hosanna!
    The Son of David see!
Lift high His royal banner,
    It is the Jubilee.

Prepare the way before Him,
    Make ready for the King;
Let all the earth adore Him,
    And costly presents bring.
Ye saints, repeat the story
    That Christ, the Lord, is come;
Sing "Hallelujah! glory!"
    And give Messiah room.

THE GUIDING STAR.

"We saw his star in the east, and are come to worship him."— Matt. 2:2.

Wise men coming from afar,
Guided by a wondrous star,
Gold and myrrh and incense bring,
Presents to the new-born King;
Worshiping they bow the knee
To His veiléd Majesty.
Lord is He of heaven and earth,
Yet He comes of lowly birth,
Not to treasure earth-prized things,
Not to rob of splendor kings,
Not a monarch's crown to take,
Nor a royal scepter break ;
But to rescue man from ill,
Working out the Father's will,
King of kings, He leaves His throne,
Clothed in flesh He walks unknown,

THE REJECTED KING.

To destroy the reign of sin,
And the reign of grace begin ;
That a mortal race might be
Raised to immortality.

BEAUTIFUL STAR.

BEAUTIFUL Star of the Orient night,
Wonderful is thy hallowed light,
Beckoning wise men from afar,
Star of the Orient, beautiful Star.

Beautiful Star, thy luminous ray
Beckoneth me along the way
To the blest Babe in Bethlehem's stall,
Born to be King and Redeemer of all.

Beautiful Star, still brightly shine,
Pointing to Jesus, the Saviour divine,
Till at His feet shall bow every knee,
Till the whole world His glory shall see.

THE FLIGHT.

"Herod will seek the young child to destroy him."—Matt. 2: 13.

Moved by jealousy and hate,
Nothing Herod's wrath could sate
But foul murder's deep-dyed stain
From the blood of infants slain.
Ah, the land of Rachel's grave!
Crushed with sorrow, none can save.
Mothers agonized are weeping
For their children's breathless sleeping.

THE REJECTED KING.

Herod's rage cannot prevail,
Nor his wily plans avail;
For the King upon the throne
Guardeth well His royal Son.
Sable Night on noiseless wings
From the East her mantle brings,
Overshading land and sea,
While the holy household flee
From the bloody murderer's hand,
From their home, their kin, their land,
To a refuge and repose
In the land of Israel's woes.

BE NOT AFRAID.

Peace, troubled soul; the Eye
  That never sleeps,
    But keeps
A faithful watch is nigh.

God's loved one need not fear;
    Wherever he
    May be,
The Father's hand is near.

His tender, loving care,
    A safe retreat,
    Complete,
Will graciously prepare.

Though hate control vain man,
    And bitter foes
    Oppose,
They only help God's plan.

In service of the Lord,
    In holy trust,
    One must
Prevail: it is God's word.

Go on then, toiling one,
    And do thy best,
    And rest
Assured, God's will is done.

THE NAZARENE.

"And he went down with them, and came to Nazareth, and was subject unto them."— Luke 2: 51.

Angels tell them, "He is dead
Whom ye feared with so much dread;"
So vile Nazareth becomes
Purest, best of earthly homes.
Here our Jesus, mirthful, mild,
Lived and sported as a child;
He who formed the virgin's frame
Her obedient Son became;
He whose hands the heavens made
Meekly human law obeyed;
He whose face was glory's sheen
Bore the name of Nazarene;
He who formed the forest tree
Wrought its wood in carpentry;
He who made the seed and soil
Won His bread by sweat and toil;

He, the Holy Son of God,
Made with sinners His abode,
Saw their vileness, shared their shame,
Felt their sorrow, bore their blame;
He who fixed the mountain's height,
Set their bounds to day and night,
O'er the hills of Galilee
Often journeyed wearily;
He who taught the herb to grow,
And the rivulet to flow,
Hungered many a weary day,
Thirsted on His toilsome way;
He who owned all earthly store,
Whom the Heavenly hosts adore,
With the poor, the weak, the lame,
To the Temple's worship came;
He who gave the wise their skill,
And the seats of power they fill,
In a child-like spirit, sweet,
Humbly questioned at their feet.

MY FATHER'S BUSINESS.

The waiting field is large and white,
And doth the sickle keen invite;
Yea, many drooping plants I see,
My Father's work is pressing me.

The reapers in the field are few
With willing hearts, and brave, and true;
Help must be summoned speedily;
My Father's work is pressing me.

The sickles rough and dull with rust,
Lie careless, trodden in the dust;
Sharpened and furbished must they be;
My Father's work is pressing me.

Let not the ripened grain be lost;
Before the winter's sleet and frost
It must be garnered faithfully;
My Father's work is pressing me.

THE PREPARATION.

*"Make ready the way of the Lord."—*Matt. 3: 3.

Era long foretold is near
When Messiah shall appear
Satan's power on earth to quell,
Jubilee of Israel.
Open wide, ye gates of day!
Death and darkness flee away!
Broken be the sway of sin!
Let the King of glory in!

John, a burning, shining light,
Like Elijah, clothed with might,
By the Holy Spirit sent,
Cometh with the words, "Repent,
Heaven's kingdom is at hand,
None before the King can stand
With His righteous, glowing ire,
With His fan and purging fire."

Breathing thoughts, in words of flame,
Stinging guilty souls with shame,
To the stern Baptizer brought
Throngs of men, who cleansing sought
Through the rite ordained to be
Type of Heavenly purity.
Their confessions, wails, distress,
Vocal made the wilderness.

THE HERALDING.

By Jordan's woody banks
  A mighty voice is heard;
From near and far, like gathering clouds,
The eager people come in crowds
  To hear the Prophet's word:
  " Behold the Lamb of God!
He comes — the nations' long desire —
He comes — a bright consuming fire —
  Behold the Lamb of God!"

The valleys, hills and wood's
And water-brooks rejoice,
The mountains hear the thrilling strain,
And echo back the grand refrain
Caught from the Preacher's voice:
"Behold the Lamb of God!
He comes to burn the chaff of sin
He comes the wheat to gather in.
Behold the Lamb of God!"

THE BAPTISM.

"And I knew him not."— John 1: 33.

Now came He who had no sin,
Fault without, or guile within,
Gentleness and love and grace
Lighting His resplendent face,
Unobserved, of humble mein,
Fairest One with mortals seen.

THE REJECTED KING.

To fulfill the law's demands
At the faithful Herald's hands.
Though the Preacher knew Him not,
Holiness without a spot
Awed the man, austere and bold,
Who the rite would fain withhold:
"I should be baptized of Thee—
Comest Thou, my Lord, to me?"
"Suffer it, and thus fulfill
God, the righteous Father's will."
   It was done at His command;
When, behold a vision grand!
Lo! the vaulted heaven rends,
Whence the Holy Ghost descends
Like a dove upon His head,
And a voice celestial said:
"This is my Beloved Son,
All my will in Him is done."
But the people, dull of ear,
Heaven's Evangel would not hear;
Blind of heart, they would not see

In the man of Galilee
Him by poets sung of old,
Him by prophets long foretold,
Israel's Saviour, Jesse's rod,
Son of David, Son of God.

JESUS COMES TO SAVE.

Behold the Lamb of God!
   He comes to save;
Behold His streaming blood!
   He comes to save.
Ye who for healing sigh,
Ye who for mercy cry,
Jesus is passing by;
   He comes to save.

THE REJECTED KING.

Ye fearful souls, draw near,
    He comes to save;
Ye dying sinners, hear,
    He comes to save.
He comes to save the lost
On raging billows tossed,
And counting not the cost,
    He comes to save.

He comes thy love to win,
    He comes to save;
He comes to conquer sin,
    He comes to save.
He comes to crush thy foe,
The path of life to show,
And rescue thee from woe;
    He comes to save.

HIS MINISTRY.

"All they in the synagogue, when they heard these things, were filled with wrath."— Luke 4: 28.

Nazareth, behold thy Guest!
Give Him welcome, and be blest ;
Lo! He seeks thy House of Prayer,
Greeting friends and neighbors where
In His youth He oft had heard
Reverently the Holy Word,
And, with deep reflection, sought
To possess the Father's thought.

The attendant gives to Him
    Isaiah's ancient Book
Of sacred visions, grand and dim.
He reads the text, returns the roll,
And sits. The fire within His soul,

THE REJECTED KING.

Like morning's radiant beam,
Makes all His features gleam.
The wondering people look
At Him with steadfast gaze, while He
Unfolds the pregnant Prophecy:

"Today this Scripture graciously
    Completed stands; the Lord
Hath to the poor anointed me
    To preach the joyful word:
To loose the captive's fettered mind
    The Spirit sendeth me,
Celestial sight to give the blind,
    And set the prisoner free;
God's time to favor men proclaim,
    And comfort them that mourn,
To take away their sin and shame,
    To heal the bruised and torn."

Lovingly He spake the word,
Jealously the people heard;

Their rebellious unbelief
Tore His gentle soul with grief,
And deserved rebuke compelled:
Foolish wrath their bosoms swelled.
Nazareth, O Nazareth!
Wilt thou put thy Lord to death?
Murder foul is in thy breast!
Heaven thy purposes arrest!
Clouds and darkness veil the place
That has banished Love and Grace!

WHERE IS JESUS?

Song of Sol. 1:7.

Where, my Beloved, canst Thou be?
O tell me, I would follow Thee.
    "Toiling at home, as Heaven wills,
    A pilgrim o'er Judean hills.

With reverent worshipers I meet,
With wise men, sitting at their feet."

Where, my Beloved, canst Thou be?
O tell me, I would follow Thee.
"Blessing the newly wedded pair,
With little children needing care,
Feeding the hungry lest they die,
Healing the blind and sick that cry."

Where, my Beloved, canst Thou be?
O tell me, I would follow Thee.
"Opening to prisoners the door,
Teaching the ignorant and poor,
Forgiving them who weep their wrong,
Filling the mourner's heart with song."

Where, my Beloved, canst Thou be?
O tell me, I would follow Thee.

"Alone all night in fervent prayer,
By Kidron's waters, weeping there,
Serenely waiting cross and grave,
Living, dying the lost to save."

THE NIGHT LONG PRAYER.

"And continued all night in prayer to God."—Luke 6: 12.

Doomed Capernaum He sought,
Where the many wonders wrought —
Sick made whole, demoniacs healed —
Power divine on earth revealed.
Wondering throngs to hear and see,
Followed Him in Galilee,
But they spurned His words so blest —
"Come, ye weary souls and rest."

THE REJECTED KING.

After toiling through the day,
Sadly Jesus turned away
To the mountain's solitude
Where no mortal might intrude.
See Him bowing to the ground,
Silence reigning all around,
Save the night bird's doleful cry,
And the breezes' moanful sigh.
What great burden weights the prayer
Of the sinless Saviour there?
While the world to slumber goes,
And disciples find repose,
While the birds and beasts repair
To their perch and covert lair,
What heart-rending sorrows roll
Over His unselfish soul?
Not a conscience in distress
From the pangs of guiltiness,
Not the fear of suffering
From the wrath of priest and king;
'Twas the chain of sinner's thrall.

'Twas the woe that whelms us all,
'Twas the direful doom impending
Over souls their God offending.

WORDS OF JESUS.

"Come hither, ye that labor,
　　With heavy burdens pressed,
My service bringeth blessing,
　　My yoke the sweetest rest."

"Behold the Rock of Ages!
　　Ye thirsty, come to me,
And drink the living water
　　That floweth full and free."

"God's love is so abounding,
　　His only Son He gave,
That whosoever willeth,
　　Eternal life shall have."

"My Father's house hath mansions,
  Both large and wondrous fair,
And when all things are ready,
  I'll come and bring you there."

O gracious words of Jesus!
  They never can grow old;
Their precious worth and sweetness
  Can never all be told.

IN SIMON'S HOUSE.

*" This man, if he were a prophet, would have perceived who
and what manner of woman this is which toucheth
him, that she is a sinner."*—Luke 7:39.

At a feast — the Pharisee's —
One to Jesus on her knees
Boweth with the guilt of years,
And His feet she bathes with tears,

Wipes them with her flowing hair,
And anoints with spikenard rare.
But the guests with haughty mein
Gaze with scorn upon the scene.
Jesus now His host addressed —
"To thy house I came a guest :
Neither water for my feet,
Nor a kiss, nor spikenard sweet
Didst thou give. This woman pours
Forth for me love's choicest stores.
Lo ! her sins are all removed,
Though so many — much she loved."

ALL FROM JESUS.

All from Jesus :
All the hope of sin forgiven,
All the comfort in life's journey,
All the promises of Heaven ;
All from Jesus.

All from Jesus;
All the vict'ries over sin,
All the strength to bear and labor,
All the help the goal to win;
All from Jesus.

All from Jesus;
All the righteousness and grace,
All the cleansing and the fitness
To behold the Father's face;
All from Jesus.

All from Jesus;
All the joy and all the trust
When the soul is winged for Heaven,
And the dust returns to dust;
All from Jesus.

All from Jesus;
All the gladness, all the song,
All the crowns and all the glory
Of that happy, blood-bought throng;
All from Jesus.

ACCUSED OF BLASPHEMY.

"And behold, certain of the scribes said within themselves, This man blasphemeth."— Matt. 9:3.

Demons know Messiah's name;
Wondering people spread His fame:
Palsied limbs and leprous skin,
Frenzied minds destroyed by sin,
Shameless souls to vice inured
By His gracious touch are cured,
Proving Him the promised Son,
Wonderful, the Mighty One.
Yet the unbelieving scribes
Cast at Him their angry gibes:
"A blasphemer," murmur they,
"Who but God takes sin away?"
All too blind to understand
He who doth disease command,
And the dying bid to live,
Can as well their sins forgive.

THE TOUCH OF JESUS.

The gracious touch of Jesus,
    So wonderful to heal,
The balm for sin and sorrow,
    Doth God in Christ reveal.

The blind who cried for mercy
    He touched, and lo! they see;
Souls held with chains of bondage
    He touched, and they are free.

The deaf who ne'er heard music
    His touch made glad with song;
The dumb who ne'er sang praises
    Rejoiced with tuneful tongue.

The withered and the dying
    He touched to noble strife;
The dead, 'mid weeping mourners,
    His touch awoke to life.

The wondrous touch of Jesus,
   So potent long ago,
Is still the one thing needful
   To save from death and woe.

AT BETHESDA.

"The Jews persecute Jesus because he did these things on the Sabbath."—John 5: 16.

'T was the Holy Sabbath day;
At Bethesda many lay,
Weak and withered, lame and blind,
Waiting anxiously to find,
In the crowd, a kindly feeling,
In the moving waters, healing.
One in pain had moaned for years,
Hoping still amid his fears.

THE REJECTED KING.

Thoughtless people hurry by,
Careless of the plaintive cry.
Jesus now is passing near—
Will He see the sufferer's tear?
Will He stoop to hear the prayer
Of the helpless in despair?
Yes, though King and Lord of all,
He will heed the humblest call.
Hear His words, so sweet and low—
"Rise, take up thy bed and go."
Lo! the impotent is whole,
Healed in body, saved in soul;
And His tongue is filled with song—
"Jesus, Jesus, made me strong."
Yet the Jews no Saviour see
In this Heavenly ministry.
Bigots blind, they seek to slay
Him who made the Sabbath day.

COME TO THE SAVIOUR.

Come, weary soul, the Saviour is calling,
    Full of compassion, and ready to save;
Come to the gracious One, trust in His word,
Come to the mighty One, He is the Lord;
Great is thy sin, but His love greater still,
Wilful thy heart is, yet stronger His will.
Come to the Saviour, come to Him now,
Come and with angels adoringly bow.

Come, needy soul, the Saviour is knocking,
    Long has He waited to enter thy door;
Open thy heart to Him, He would come in,
Give thy best room to Him, turn out thy sin;
Though thou hast wronged Him, His pardon is free,
Though thou hast slighted, His feast waiteth thee.
Come to the Saviour, come to Him now,
Come and with angels adoringly bow.

THE REJECTED KING. 43

Come, sinful soul, the Saviour is waiting,
   Patient and loving and ready to save;
Say to the waiting One, "Here is my heart,"
Say to the loving One, "My Lord Thou art."
Tell all thy sin to Him, He will forgive,
Tell all thy love to Him, He will receive.
Come to the Saviour, come to Him now,
Come and with angels adoringly bow.

BLASPHEMED.

"*By Beelzebub the prince of the devils casteth he out devils.*"—Luke 11: 15.

Our Father in Heaven, be hallowed Thy name,
The world, as Thy kingdom, now speedily claim,
Thy will, as with angels, be done here, we pray,
The bread that is needful, O give us each day.
Forgive our transgressions as we now forgive,
Exposed to temptation, O may we not live,
But save from the Evil One, Father divine,
For kingdom and power and glory are Thine.

While this prayer the Saviour taught,
One possessed to Him was brought,
Sinful, wretched, blind and dumb,
By foul demons overcome.
Through His word the man was healed
And the power of God revealed;
But the people blindly said —
"Jesus heals through Satan's aid."

Jewish hearts with hate were filled,
Sweetly love from His distilled.
"A deceiver," murmured they,
But of truth He was the way;
In His life was nothing wrong,
"He hath devils," cried the throng;
While he labored for their good,
They were thirsting for His blood.

THE LOVE OF JESUS.

The love of Jesus, O how free!
    A boundless sea!
Embracing all, below, above,
    The sea of love.

It reaches far as sin is found,
    And wrongs abound,
And man is saved, without, within,
    From guilt and sin.

Oh, shoreless ocean, deep and broad!
    The love of God!
The ruined tribes of every race
    May trust thy grace.

The world redeemed by Thee shall raise
    The song of praise,
And join with all the hosts above
    To tell Thy love.

ESCAPED FROM THE STONING.

"They took up stones therefore to cast at him, but Jesus hid himself." — John 8:59.

Brought by Pharisee and scribe,
With a haughty, heartless gibe,
Once a woman in disgrace
Cow'red before the Saviour's face
In confusion, guilty, vile.
Her accusers full of guile,
Proving her in sin, invite
Him to tell them what was right.
"What say'st Thou? The law is plain
Stoned until the sinner's slain."
But their craft and guilt He saw,
And the wretched woman's awe,
And, for them with shame profound,
Stooped and wrote upon the ground.
Urged, He spake — incensed within —

"Let the person free from sin
Be the first to cast a stone."
Self-condemned they, one by one,
Stole away, as culprits will,
Stung by conscious guilt, until
Misery and Mercy rare
Face to face were standing there.
Jesus saw the contrite tear,
Knew that humble heart sincere,
And He said with accents mild
To the now believing child.
"Go thy way and sin no more"—
Word, like Moses' rod of yore,
Giving drink to Israel's flock
From the desert's smitten rock —
"Go thy way, from sin depart,"
Smote the fountain of her heart.
"Not condemned to endless gloom,"
For the Morning Star has come,
Light in darkness, Heavenly flame,
Making glad a soul of shame.

Jesus said, "I am the light
Of the world, no cheerless night
Can becloud their shining way
Who observe me and obey."
Many words of truth profound,
To the multitude around,
From His heart — a fountain stored —
Like a river Jesus poured;
While the stream of wisdom flowed,
All His radiant features glowed.
But the Jews with anger burned,
And His words of life they spurned;
Seizing stones they sought to slay
Christ, the Life, the Truth, the Way, —
But He vanished out of sight;
Leaving them in wilful night.

THE MIND OF JESUS.

The mighty works of Jesus
    Along His rugged way,
Like fountains in the desert,
    His gracious mind display:
So I will follow Jesus
    Among the poor and blind,
Beseeching Him to give me
    The same unselfish mind.

Behold Him with the lepers,
    The palsied and the lame!
He leaves them all rejoicing
    And publishing His name.
O for the mind of Jesus,
    His love and gentleness,
His grace and sweet compassion,
    His pity for distress!

Now moved by weeping mourners
    He gives them back their dead;
And hungry thousands thronging
    By Him are freely fed.
O for the mind of Jesus,
    His faithfulness and zeal,
His patience and His mercy,
    His love for all men's weal!

O blessed mind of Jesus!
    O love beyond compare!
I cannot know its fulness,
    But let this be my prayer:
"His spirit meek and lowly,
    His sweet humility,
His purpose, high and holy,
    O give them, Lord, to me!"

BESOUGHT TO DEPART.

"They besought him that he would depart from their borders."
Matt. 8:34.

Daylight now is growing dim;
Yet new throngs are pressing Him.
Teaching on the sea-chafed shore —
His own temple's pebbly floor.
Calling His disciples, He
Bids them come and cross the sea,
While the night on silent wings,
Darkness deep around them brings.
Worn with toil He seeks for rest,
And with slumber deep is blest.

Suddenly a tempest comes;
Lo! the angry water foams.
The disciples fearing, cry —
" Master, save us, or we die."

Now sublime amid the storm
Stands serene that noble form,
While He utters — "Peace, be still."
Winds and waves obey His will.
As the billows of the sea
Know His voice and instantly
Bow obedient to His word,
Will not man confess Him Lord?

Gergesa swing wide thy gates,
Jesus at thy portal waits.
Now thy favored hour is come,
Give the great Messiah room!
List! a frenzied madman raves
From the tombs in rocky caves.
Fierce, by demon power possessed,
Yet he knows this God-like Guest,
And he runs to meet the Lord,
Prostrate falling at the word —
"Out from him thou spirit vile,
Quit the soul thou dost defile."

"Legion" was the demon's name,
From that soul the legion came;
And the man in freedom sweet
Sat restored at Jesus' feet.
When these things, so strange, were heard
In the city, all were stirred,
And with folly in their heart
Urged the Saviour to depart.
Gergesa, O Gergesa!
Under what ill-omened star
Dost thou mourn thy herd of swine,
And reject the Lord Divine?

THE REJECTED KING.

AT THE FEET OF JESUS.

At the feet of Jesus,
    Place of pardon sweet,
Sinners, lost and guilty,
    Here compassion meet.

At the feet of Jesus
    Sheltered well I hide;
Sin can never harm me
    While I here abide.

At the feet of Jesus
    Do I learn to be
Reaper in the harvest
    For eternity.

At the feet of Jesus
    Joyfully I wait
Till the Master bid me,
    Enter Heaven's gate.

AT BETHANY.

"From that day forth they took counsel together to put him to death."—John 11: 53.

Bethany, sweet Bethany,
One dear home has hallowed thee,
Loved by Him whose love is more
Than far Ophir's golden store.
Here the King oft turned for rest,
Here three loving souls were blest ;
Theirs to serve with tender care ;
His, to pour out wisdom rare.

Martha, much with care encumbered
   Served her honored Lord ;
Mary's hours were sweetly numbered
   Listening to His word ;
Martha, making toil her pleasure,
   Pleased her noble Guest ;
Mary, pouring out love's treasure,
   Pleased her Master best.

While their Friend was far away,
An unbidden guest, one day,
Forced an entrance to their cot —
Lazarus, alas! was not.
All the grief of hearts so true,
Hopes defeated, Jesus knew,
Saw the solemn train and bier,
Farewell kiss and scalding tear,
Knew the brother's mortal sleep,
Came to comfort and to weep.

"The Master is come, and calleth for thee,
Fear not, weeping child, His love thou shalt see.
He feels for thy grief, He bears all thy blows,
He weeps for thy tears, and carries thy woes;
Arise from thy couch and speed to the place
Where Jesus doth wait to show thee His grace.
Thy prayer shall be heard if thou wilt believe,
Great things God will give if thou canst receive."

At the grave He breathed a groan:
When they rolled away the stone,

With up lifted eyes to Heaven —
" Father, Thou hast answer given
To my prayer, and I rejoice : "
Then He cried with mighty voice :
" Lazarus, come forth ! " and he
That was dead lived instantly.
 For these acts of mercy shown,
Miracles of grace well known —
Mourners solaced, hungry fed,
Blind restored, and raised the dead —
Jewish priest and Pharisee
Were but filled with enmity :
And, in secret counsel, they
All agreed the Christ to slay.

JESUS WHISPERS.

When thy breast
Heavily with care is pressed,
  Jesus whispers tenderly,
  " Come to me,
I will give the weary rest."

When thy soul
Bleeds in pain at sin's control,
  Jesus whispers graciously,
  " Look to me,
I will make the wounded whole."

When draw near
Dread forebodings, dark and drear,
  Jesus whispers lovingly,
  " Trust in me,
I will take away thy fear."

When Death's night
Darkness spreads o'er mortal sight,
Jesus whispers faithfully,
" Lean on me,
I will give thee life and light."

WEEPING OVER JERUSALEM.

"And when he drew nigh, he saw the city, and wept over it."
Luke 19: 41.

BEHOLD Him that cometh by prophets foretold!
The way strown with garments and branches behold!
With shouts of hozanna the mountain tops ring;
His march is triumphal, He cometh a King.
Though meekly He rides on the symbol of peace,
Approaching the city, the shoutings increase —
"Hozanna, hozanna to David's great Son!
For great are the deeds the Anointed hath done."
But O, how amazing! the King is in tears
While shining in splendor the city appears;
As shouts from the lips of the multitude leap,

The doom of fair Salem compels Him to weep:
"If thou, O Jerusalem, only couldst see
The day of thy peace! But 'tis hidden from thee.
Too late will be weeping to save thee from woe,
Rejecting thy Friend thou shalt fall by thy foe."

As a hen her chickens brings
To the covert of her wings,
So Jerusalem, would I,
Gathering my children nigh,
Guard them from the wrath to come,
Shield them from impending doom;
But they will not come to me,
To my refuge will not flee.
"O perverse Jerusalem!
Thou that blindly killest them
Sent to thee in Mercy's name,
Thy redemption to proclaim!
O Jerusalem, alas!
Soon thy woes shall come to pass!
And thy house, so famed and great,
Shall be left thee desolate.

JESUS, ADVOCATE.

Jesus, Advocate unseen,
Me and judgment just between,
What I am and what I've been
   Thou canst see, Lord, Thou canst see.

Every sinful word and thought,
Every selfish object sought,
Every failure I have wrought,
   Pardon me, O, pardon me.

All my help when woes prevail,
All my hope when earth shall fail,
All my trust when sinners quail
   Are in Thee, Lord, are in Thee.

To Thy judgment when I come,
Stand between my soul and doom,
With the righteous give me room
   Graciously, O, graciously.

THE LAST SUPPER.

"This is my body which is given for you."— Luke 22:19

All made ready for the feast,
Bread and wine and slaughtered beast,
Jesus and His friends repair
To the Paschal supper, where
Type and Antitype complete
In that sacred chamber meet.
Now, O shame! before His face
His disciples strive for place:
But their King, through love uncrowned,
With a servant's napkin bound,
Stoops to wash their weary feet,
Soiled and heated in the street.
When such humbleness we see,
What is our humility?
When such love as His is seen,
What's our love but semblance mean?

THE REJECTED KING.

After the Paschal Lamb was eat.
Wine-cups filled and drank, they yet
Linger on His words, while He,
Down the centuries to be,
Doth with prophet-vision gaze,
And decree, to their amaze,—
" Let the broken bread and wine
Be a sacrament divine,
Symbols of my flesh and blood,
Offered up for you to God;
Bond of brotherhood and love,
Pledge of fellowship above,
Feast, forevermore to be
A memorial of me."

Was there in that company
One so sunk in infamy,
One, whose false and selfish soul
Was so under sin's control,
That he did not, could not share
In that entertainment rare?

That he could not have a part
In that fellowship of heart?
Speed him from that holy place
Where our God unveils His face!
Darkness, hide the traitor's tracks!
Mortals, tremble for his acts!

REMEMBER ME.

Remember Thee, dear Lord!
    Can I forget the love
That brought Thee down to weeping earth
    From Thy blest courts above?

Can I forget Thy sweat
    And toil in Galilee?
Thy weariness at Sychar's well,
    Thy great humility?

Can I forget Thy hand
    Laid gently on my head,
And "Let the little children come,"
    So kindly, sweetly said?

Forget Thou saidst to me —
    Unused to love before —
When all my sin and guilt were known,
    "Go, child, and sin no more?"

Can I forget Thy look
    In Pilate's judgment hall,
When scourged and mocked and crowned with thorns,
    And wounded by my fall?

Can I forget Thy cross,
    And agonizing cry —
"My God, why dost Thou hide from me?"
    "Lama Sabachthani?"

GETHSEMANE.

"*My soul is exceeding sorrowful even unto death.*"— Mark 14 : 34.

It is night. The traitor goes
Stealthily to Jesus foes,
Plotting with them to betray
Christ before the dawn of day.
After their last supper ends,
Still He lingers with His friends,
Comforting them tenderly
Ere He seeks Gethsemane.
 From that sacred upper room
Come they to the Garden's gloom.
Many woes had Jesus known,
Meekly bearing them alone;
Many conflicts had He met,
But the greatest conflict yet
Was to be endured in thee,
O thou sad Gethsemane!

Crushed with sorrow strange and deep,
His disciples drowned in sleep,
Heedless e'en the chosen three,
Dead all human sympathy.
Kneeling, weeping there alone,
See Him wrestle, hear Him groan,
Witness ye His agony,
Stones of mute Gethsemane!
See His visage marred and wet
With great drops of bloody sweat!
"O my Father, if thou be
Willing, take this cup from me:
Yet Thy will, not mine be done,"
Prayed the meek, obedient Son.
Who may solve the mystery
Of that dark Gethsemane?
Tell me what malignant dart
Had so pierced the Saviour's heart.
'Twas not fear that made Him cry,
Nor the death He was to die;
For, to bear the cross, He came.

With its cruelty and shame.
Whence, then, came His agony
'Neath thy shade, Gethsemane?
  Had the tempter, armed for fight,
Come again in dreadful might?
Had the Father hid His face
From the Friend of such a race,
Leaving Death and horrid gloom
Free to make this world a tomb!
Was the weight of human guilt
Crumbling this fair temple built
Of material too frail,
So His mission here might fail,
And mankind bewail the loss
If He died not on the cross?
Man may never, never know
All the depths of Jesus' woe;
But the Son shall victor be
Even in Gethsemane.

Heaven heard the suppliant prayer,
Angels flew to help Him there;
And He calmly met the band
Led by Judas' guilty hand,
Saying, "Let us go, behold
Now is come the hour foretold."
With divine sublimity
Jesus left Gethsemane.

JESUS ALONE.

O Saviour, can it be
    That I can sleep,
Whilst Thou in bitter agony
    Dost pray and weep!

To watch Thou calledst me
    For Thy dear sake;
But slumber presses heavily,
    I cannot wake.

THE REJECTED KING.

"No, cannot watch one hour,"
  With shame I cry;
And Satan with malignant power
  Is pressing nigh.

Lord Jesus, Thou the blow
  Must bear alone;
Alone must face man's mighty foe
  And weep and groan.

BETRAYAL AND TRIAL.

"They shouted, saying, crucify, crucify him."— Luke 23:21.

Judas comes — the traitor seen
In his heartless kiss and mein —
With a crowd equipped with arms,
'Neath the shade of leaf-crowned palms.
Terror-stricken at the sight
His disciples cower in flight.

THE REJECTED KING. 71

Like a felon, bound with cord,
Soldiers lead away the Lord.
　Now before their Council vile,
Marked by bitter hate and guile,
Jesus stands in Judgment Hall,
Mocked, condemned, despised by all;
Though in Heavenly counsel high
He had given Himself to die
To redeem the world from woe,
And its tyrant overthrow.
Priest and elders, mad and blind,
Seek false witnesses to find
To condemn by law the right,
And with darkness hide the light.
Love and mercy are belied,
Truth and justice are denied;
Yet, how strange! He answers not
To their perjured slanders brought.
When adjured by priest to say
Whether He was Christ or nay,
Jesus said. "I am, and ye

Soon the Son of Man shall see
Seated at the Father's side,
Clothed with power, though now decried;
Coming to the earth again,
Robed in cloud and crowned to reign."
"Blasphemy," the rulers cried;
"Guilty," every voice replied.
Author of abounding grace,
Sinners smite Thee on the face.
Thou who gav'st these wretches breath,
Art by them condemned to death.
Now to Pilate He was brought,
Then by Herod set at naught.
Scoffed, reviled by servile bands,
Rudely scourged by soldiers' hands;
But their scorn He meekly bore,
And their crown of insult wore,
While they, jeering, bowed the knee,
Hailing Him in irony.
"Crucify Him, crucify!"
Was their fierce and angry cry:

"Let the murderer go free,
Let Barabbas pardoned be,
But to death let Christ be led,
And His blood be on our head."

Of humaneness all bereft,
Lost the man — the savage left,
What had filled their hearts with hate?
What was His offense so great,
That His blood, and nothing less,
Must now sate their bitterness?
That a cross of crimson dye
Must their rancor satisfy?

Hear Ye:
   Jesus has been tried
At the bar of maddened pride,
And the cause of His offense
Found to be His innocence,
Nobleness and virtue pure,
Truth which sin cannot endure.

Wisdom with humility,
Pow'r not used vaingloriously.
Holiness begot above,
And for sinners *too much love.*

THE CRUCIFIXION.

"*And they crucified him, and the malefactors.*"— Luke 23: 33.

As it was in Bethlehem —
" In the inn no room for them "—
So forever has it been ;
Room for suffering and sin,
Room for passion, room for vice,
Room for human sacrifice,
Room for hatred, room for pride,
Room for falsehood to abide,

THE REJECTED KING.

Room for masters and their slaves,
Room for battles, room for graves,
Room for selfishness and greed,
Room for broken hearts to bleed;
But for Truth and Love and Grace,
In the world was found no place;
None for Him who came to save
But a Golgotha and grave.
Room at last, ye angels see!
Room is found on Calvary!
Room for jagged nail and spear!
Room for groans! O Heaven, hear!
Room for blood and ghastly wounds!
Room for grief that has no bounds!
Room for Jesus on the tree!
Room to die in agony!
Let the sun refuse to shine
On the Sufferer Divine!
Wrong has triumphed over right!
Darkness over Heaven's light!

Rend ye rocks, ye mountains quake!
From your dust ye saints awake!
For in Joseph's rock-hewn tomb
Man's Redeemer lies in gloom.
Long and dark the night must be!
Who beyond its shade can see?
Faith, the legacy of ages,
Hope, inspirer of the sages,
Star, that led from Orient lands,
Advent song of angel bands,
Promises to prophets made,
In a sealed tomb are laid.

Grace is spurned and God blasphemed;
All of which the ancients dreamed,
Poets sang in verse profound,
Men have trampled to the ground.
Yet, no wrath of God awakes,
Ne'er a sound His silence breaks,
Patient and forbearing still,
Love controls His dreadful will.

Day for them is calm and fair,
Still they breathe the fragrant air,
Draw their food from land and main,
Whose Creator they have slain.
Beautiful the moon at night
Pours for them its silver light ;
Freighted clouds on snowy wings
Store for them refreshing springs.
O the wondrous love of God!
Like the ocean, deep and broad,
Patient and forbearing still,
Mercy holds His fateful will ;
His dread hand He lifteth not
From His book their names to blot,
Though His Son they've crucified,
Spurned His Gifts, His grace denied.

THE RESURRECTION.

*"He Himself stood in the midst of them." "Peace be
unto you.— Luke 24:36.*

Lo, the tomb of rock is shaking!
Through its gloom a light is breaking!
Seal and stone and guard are vain.
Sin and Death by Christ are slain.
Faith is realized in sight,
Hope in joys with glory bright,
For that star the Sun appears,
Easter-song the mourner cheers.
Jesus lives! and hearts are glad
Late with keenest sorrow sad ;
Jesus lives! and, wondrous grace,
Meets His loved ones face to face,
Joins them in their gloomy walk,
Comforts while they sadly talk,
Opens to their minds the word,
Shows Himself their risen Lord.

When disciples meet for prayer
He mysteriously is there,
And their doubts all disappear,
Peace prevails and Heaven is near.
By His frequent presence blest
They believe their wondrous Guest
Always near, in union sweet,
Wedlock holy and complete,
Whom they feel and seem to see
In their joyful company,
Radiant before their eyes,
Though ascended to the skies.

Their Messiah — veiled from sight —
Yet is with them in His might;
And the message they have heard
From His lips, "Go preach my word
To all nations far and near,"
They obey without a fear,
On His promise they depend,
" I am with you to the end."

Hasten, Pentecostal hour!
Holy Ghost, display Thy power!
Wonders work in Jesus' name!
Mortals speak with tongues of flame!
Sinners, for your hardness, grieve!
Thousands in a day believe!
Let the guilty race draw near,
Love's forgiving voice to hear!
Let the nations, lost and blind,
Come, and their Redeemer find!
Prisoners, drop your chains and sing—
"Glory, glory to the King!"
Darkness, flee before the light!
Demons, speed your swiftest flight!
From his throne let Death be hurled!
Let Christ's kingdom fill the world!

JESUS IN THE MIDST.

In the midst of Eden's bowers,
'Mid perennial fruits and flowers,
Bloomed the Tree of Life most fair —
'Twas a type of Jesus there.

In the midst of seraphs prone
Reverently around the throne,
Is the Lamb for sinners slain —
Type of Him who lives to reign.

In the soul where Jesus reigns,
More than Eden's bliss obtains;
Flowerets there forever blow;
There celestial harvests grow.

Where disciples meet to pray
Jesus rules with gentle sway,
Filling every heart and tongue
With the Lamb's adoring song.

ROOM FOR JESUS.

"Behold I stand at the door and knock."— Rev. 3: 20

Nations, give Emmanuel room;
Not a cross — the felon's doom,
Not a grave of gathering mold,
Not a prison, dark and cold:
Give Him valley, hill and mountain,
Give Him sea and stream and fountain,
Give Him flocks and corn and gold,
Give Him treasures new and old,
Give Him temple, church and hall,
Give Him palace, cottage, stall,
Let His banner be unfurled
Through the kingdom of the world.
Congregations, give Him room:
Not a gilded, marble tomb,
Not a place 'mid hearts of ice
Not a seat with honored vice,

THE REJECTED KING.

Give Him room, though scarred and fettered,
Awkward, homely and unlettered;
Room for Him, swing wide the door
Though He enters with the poor;
Bid Him welcome, though He comes
Dressed in rags from wretched homes;
Let Him come in every race,
Trophies of redeeming grace.
Christian household, give Christ room
Let Him to your table come,
At your altar when you kneel,
His blest presence may you feel;
When you wake and when you sleep,
Let His love your treasures keep;
Where your children work or play,
Urge this Heavenly Guest to stay;
With your neighbors when you meet,
Give to Him the choicest seat;
Greatly will that house be blest
Which shall give to Him its best.

Hark thee, soul! a Friend has come;
He is knocking, give Him room.
He would enter at thy door,
Though 'tis dusty, rough and poor;
Bid Him welcome to abide;
Where He dwells He will provide,
Peace and plenty He will bring,
He that knocketh is thy King.
He would sup with thee tonight,
But tomorrow may invite
Thee to be His favored guest
In the mansions of the blest.

SOUL, ARISE!

Soul, arise! and give Christ room;
Not alone thy days of gloom;
Not when sinks the setting sun;
Not when all thy work is done.

Give thy brightest, noblest powers;
Give thy purest, sweetest hours,
Give thy will, thy mind, thy heart;
Give to Jesus all thou art.

Then 'twill be His time to give
More than mortals can conceive;
Rooms within His mansions fair,
Where all precious blessings are.

Room for Jesus, give Him room,
Open wide each heart and home!
Let His banner be unfurled
Through the kingdoms of the world!

THE BELIEVER'S RESPONSE.

Out of my bondage, sorrow and night,
Into Thy freedom, gladness and light;
Out of my sickness into Thy health,
Out of my want and into Thy wealth,
Out of my sin and into Thyself,
Jesus, I come; Jesus, I come.

Out of my shameful failure and loss,
Into the glorious gain of Thy cross;
Out of earth's poisons into Thy balm,
Out of life's storms into Heavenly calm,
Out of distress into jubilant psalm,
Jesus, I come; Jesus, I come.

Out of unrest and arrogant pride,
Into Thy restful will to abide;

THE REJECTED KING. 87

Out of myself to dwell in Thy love,
Out of despair into raptures above,
Upward for aye on wings of a dove,
Jesus, I come; Jesus, I come.

Out of my death and th' shade of the tomb,
Into Thy life and beauteous home;
Out of the depths of ruin untold,
Into the cheer of Thy sheltered fold,
Into the streets and city of gold,
Jesus, I come; Jesus, I come.

www.ingramcontent.com/pod-product-compliance
Lightning Source LLC
Chambersburg PA
CBHW020159170426
43199CB00010B/1104